JOHN LATHAM CANVAS EVENTS

Ridinghouse

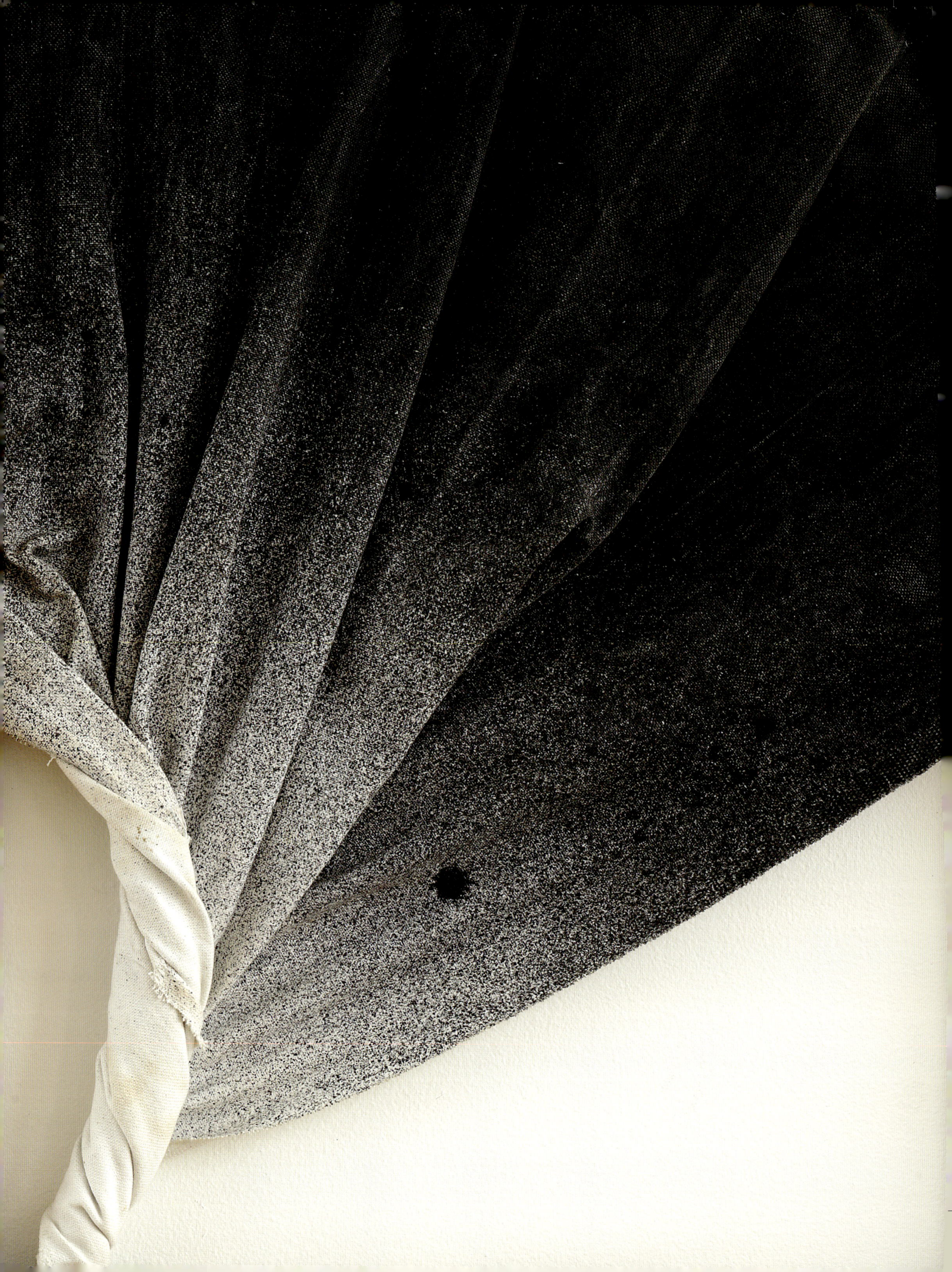

'I make the world and the world makes me'

John Latham in conversation with Hans Ulrich Obrist and Barbara Steveni

In this conversation we are talking about a work, the last in a series which identifies the universe as an 'event' as being 'event-structured', and now called 'Flat Time'. The series started with an unmarked white surface which, following an exhibition of Robert Rauschenberg (1951), declared (my interpretation) '(all) art is on par with zero action'. The conclusion of a century-long shift in art is seen as a shift in thought dynamics from a spatially based world view to one which is event-structured. The series proceeds from the collapsed history state with a rapid accretion of black point marks as made by a spray can on a white surface. The surface now registers a consistent history of itself and an abstract of former histories. The series proceeded through the use of other actions as painting but retaining this concept of a consistent history in the *now* state. We are looking at a typical constellation here, and using it to demonstrate a way of picturing a present day map where an organism such as ourselves is present as a body-event having a 'half-life' or reproductive frequency represented by a vertical line along a *Time-Base Spectrum*. This T-B Spectrum line stretches from the shortest regularity in nature to the longest (where we are looking at one universal cycle). The T-B Spectrum is now a horizontal line having a width, which we see as a turning cylinder from which a canvas unrolls. A 'drop' of the canvas as it unrolls is 'time' and 'count', as with clocks. The roller as a work in itself displays three time-related components of a universe in which the characteristics of a *Reflective Intuitive Organism* (*RIO)* are all present within the whole span of the universe, from quantum unit to one complete enactment. The use in the video of a constellatory 'blob' is intended to show the pragmatic potential for mapping states of being within a single principle of order, an information system where the longer time-base determines the order of the shorter, anywhere the shortest is found (by physical science) to be the most determined, what they call mass-energy and so on. We from the art track are looking here not at appearances but at sources of action.

Hans Ulrich Obrist

Canvas Event [4], 1994 (detail)

JOHN LATHAM If I move this from ... if I have the blob there that is an aggregate of information. The information is on that line and on that line – the 'P' line is the body event of the person. Most people's imagination circulates around what that body is. If the centre of gravity of that is moved slightly to the right, it comes into contact with something which is intellectually more interesting. The greater interest becomes a 'Q' – the 'Q' band society is the one we have today, the highly democratised or the highly organised society. And if you then push that across to the 'R' band, it's touching the intuition which can reorganise, recast the language because the language has got built into it, a flaw which makes us go back to that state. It's just a coincidence that the two pieces are made, but I would use them in a lecture if I was talking to students, just to show what the scope is, because all this is sources of information which have a specific point in drop-time going down that way [points to left-hand axis] and it's 'count or clock' time. That is the time base along there which has got the impulse, you see, is in this coordinate. And, of course, the square of it is the invisible world which is always there and it's a platonic part of the world that doesn't change, and it comes from some previous Greek philosopher, Parmenides, who was well-known for it, and it's stayed within physics. And there's a wonderful book *Science and the Modern World*, by Whitehead, published in 1925 as lectures arguing that we must start from the 'event' as the unit.

HANS ULRICH OBRIST I have several questions about archives and books in relation to your work on them. The first question is obviously very basic, how you started to use books in your work, to begin from the beginning ...

BARBARA STEVENI That would be very good and I could flash back and get that book on, you know, the sculpture from Pittsburgh which has your things on the front.

JL Partly what I'd say to Hans Ulrich is that very fast use of the spray gun began an archive of the universe which was what the cosmological people, what those two scientists, were out to construct. If psycho-physical cosmology, let's say a cosmology which did not have the kind of people that we know, but the reflective intuitive organism – to use my terms – the organism that becomes reflective, intuitive and capable is built in to a flat time universe coming from these forms, so that is basically the archive, where the books make a reflective intuitive organism universe. You'd see that in one of the series of 17 panels in the catalogue which I showed Chris Isham. He said, 'this is what we're doing in the college just now ... two kinds of time.' And the same thing could be said of these images, there you can get that on to the focus, those two states where the focus and mass, the mass of the black when tracked across the grid shows the difference between an organism which is a plague, which is a sort of E. coli.

HUO What you mentioned in your ...

JL A parasitic organism kills its host and the other one ... And the other one has unknown potentiality because it's aware of how to follow what its proper destiny might be and it's probably not spatial.

HUO But is it in this sense a kind of a symbiotic archive? Kisha Kowokawa talks about symbiotic architecture in terms of the Japanese metabolism, the whole Japanese architecture metabolism.

JL I am not familiar with the Japanese architecture.

HUO But the symbiotic notion, how would you see this in relation to your work?

JL Well, one doesn't have to use symbiotic as a word. It's automatic that the event which constructs the architecture would know that for example concrete vegetables, if they're in the form of concrete vegetables, they are very ephemeral in paleological time and it's not very useful to use the word 'symbiotic' when the interest is that the two together are the one event. The important event is the two together: the one sets up the site for the other. There is a Latin tag which the scientists had, *Mundum facio, mundo*.

BS What does it mean?

JL I just remember it coming out in the magazine which they produced, 'I make the world, and the world makes me'.

BS That's lovely.

HUO Yes. When physically for the first time do books appear in your work? What was the very first appearance of books?

JL Yes, well, if I was to tell that story. Shall I tell that story?

BS Yes, can we ...

JL Well, let me just carry on from there because ...

BS ... and the dots and the marks.

JL The people who are interested in this little story would know that having invented – because nobody else had ever used it – the point marks of a spray-painting machine and used them as black on white, which is mathematically commensurate, revealed many images of the development of a human being within it. When that was exhausted I found that what I'd needed was a surface which was less flat. So I was looking for something, really, which would serve as another form and I came across a piece of corrugated asbestos stuff which people use to make roofs and I thought, well, this is useful, this is interesting as a wave form as it's got continuity in the form of waves. And of course the simplest thing to do with that was to get it back to flat and I thought, well, I can use the idea of plaster and glass and get the glass to make a flat surface on top of the wave so that it would be comparable. The next thing I did was to see a book on the table and the book immediately spoke as being white with black marks on it, just like the thing which I'd been doing previously. And the fact that the white marks, the white page was condensed, the information coded from the constellatory world picture which we'd invented there had turned into black marks which were all in a known code, so that we had tracked ourselves into an extended time 'reading' event. And when that extended time event was put into sculptural space it stood for 'non-extended' time, there's a 'non-extended' time in art presentation on the two dimensional surface.

Visual art is supposed to be non-moving. It's the best thing about it. As you and I can move in all kinds of ways, the thing which is flat and doesn't move is more fundamental than movies. Well, it gradually developed into a mapping of what people do when they are automatic, when they're ordinary organisms and behaving according to instructions inside one book. In biology a genetic code. And if they have access to another source in another book storing in another code a reasoning of what the automatic behaviour brings about, then they begin to change their own behaviour. If they then become too clever in that, become intellectually too clever, they fail to get any new information. It's like having the whole world computerised. Everybody will follow the computer but the computer won't have access to what intuition can reach ...

BS Hence the burning of books to draw attention to this loaded language and ...

JL Yes ... I've not yet finished with this particular story because it must end. The key to the artist in the organism, the social organism, is that the intuition of the artist isn't verbally driven; it comes out without there being a reason for it. It's totally unscripted and probably regarded as destructive, as subversive – riff-raff, as it's been called. I had a lot of come back from it; the official response was to stop it. I had this very interesting show in Oxford where the students flocked around the exhibition ...

HUO What year was that?

JL That was 1963. The students loved it and there were reports on it. There was an article in *The Guardian* about it, but the staff, the academics were really against it. They launched a movement to get it obscured, deleted.

HUO Why didn't they like it?

JL Well first of all it's very bad for writers, and they say it's a very bad example for the young to tear up books and to burn them. Well, that is an assault on the whole of what we regard as value, the value of the past and ...

HUO The whole academic establishment in England was disturbed by your Greenberg event ...

BS Absolutely.

HUO Could you tell us something about this?

JL Yes, the Greenberg thing. Well, Barry Flanagan and I were in St Martin's School of Art. I was on the staff and Barry was asking me when we talked whether there [was] something we could do together and said, 'Well, we could do a little performance at home.' And eventually we sent out some invitations to a 'Still and Chew' party. 'Still' meant the intended distillation, which was hidden, and the 'Chew' sounded like eating. Well, they were then presented with the Greenberg book and asked to choose a page to chew and spit it out into a flask.

HUO What year was that?

JL That was 1967, I think. In 1966 we had the 'Chew' and then in 1967 ... the librarian didn't ask for the book back until almost a year later and by that time I'd had it distilling away, actually. I got together a little flask and put it together with the postcard which said, '*Art and Culture* wanted urgently by a student. Please return your overdue book.' I brought it in and she said, 'Well, what's this?' And I said, 'This is the book that you asked for.' She said, 'Oh, well I'm waiting for the book. I want the book.' And I said, 'Yes, the student that you mentioned – give him this and ...'

HUO Fantastic.

JL She said, 'Oh, people want to, people need to read these things.' I said, 'Well, if that's all you have to say, then that's all you have to say. I mean, take it and put it in the space where the book goes.'

HUO Did they archive it or did they throw it away?

BS It's in the Museum of Modern Art.

HUO This I know. But that's the distilled book you handed over to the librarian. That's the piece which is in the Museum of Modern Art?

BS The piece that ... Yes, it's got the 'wanted urgently by a student'. So it's got that. It's got the little ...

JL The phial and all the documents are in a correspondence case, set out as an exhibit.

BS All the documents that related to that event. The invitation, everything is in a little box called *'Art and Culture'*.

HUO And you were subsequently sacked from the art school because of this?

JL Yes ... I got this letter saying, 'I'm sorry, I can't invite you to do any more teaching.' And everybody laughed.

[Laughter]

JL It gave great pleasure to me. I mean that was enough ... But then there was a critic called Lawrence Alloway, wasn't it? Or Lucy Lippard? Lucy Lippard got wind of it and ... Yes, she presented it in her *Information* show which introduced 'Art as Concept'. She took it to San Francisco, to the Art Critics' Conference in San Francisco, and sent me a postcard saying it was voted their favourite piece.

BS Sarrat says it's the piece he uses as Conceptual art, absolutely making a statement, so he also uses that piece as his favourite conceptual work ...

JL It was totally fortuitous. I hadn't planned it at all.

BS And you hadn't planned being sacked either.

JL I hadn't planned being sacked. I just took it for what happened. Actually, I knew that they would buy it because it was all going so well. They'd bought one before, the museum had bought a thing which had been taken across to them before and they'd said, 'Oh, this is very unusual, we've never seen anything like this. We'd better have it.' They hung it next to Rauschenberg's 'combine' of the day – it was a good sort of ad-type event.

BS Yes, but that was so shocking compared to, say, the *Sensation* show, because it's very interesting that what shocked at that time was absolutely suppressed because it was seen in terms of the burned etc. books, as anarchy. And the whole of what we did as artists, anything that we did after that in our social way getting a proper kind of role for the artist to take up relative to commercial organisation. None of the art world or the art establishment could talk about any of it because it all related back to the anarchic movement of destruction in art. So, when anything came up to the art establishment at that time it was suppressed and, so it wasn't until the 'Out of actions' shows that this interest came through and people started looking at it.

HUO And now with a new generation, these ideas are revisited.

BS And the new generation are really interested so that, when I take the archives – to move on to your archives – which are going into the Tate the students, the MA course at Goldsmiths said, APG or O+I must not put this history into the Tate, into an institution because the institutions have been so opposed to new ideas in this country, unless the actual artist's voice comes out. And therefore they wanted to make the archive a living sculpture, which is how Barry came into it and how he made this presentation.

HUO Can you tell me a little bit how you archive things ...

JL I don't.

BS The interesting thing is that everybody is crawling across to try and get the precious bits and documents of John, and in doing the APG archive, of course, all this stuff is coming out. And what is needed now is a person who is going to pull out the archives and do this, because John does not archive. He's too much in the present.

HUO So you were never interested in archiving your own ...

BS Not at all, never.

JL Well, I made a list, I made a list ...

HUO From distillation of books to not doing your own archives, there is a kind of a direct link.

BS Yes, there's never been any concern that anything was precious, to be contained. Because I have always felt with John and with myself, the motivation is: what does this mean, and what are we doing now? So it's always in the present, but the past has been extraordinarily interesting. But it's always the motivation behind what it all means and what one's doing with one's life. So I mean John has never archived anything. Nicholas Logsdail was saying, well, you know, I mean Joseph Beuys's – just a little piece of paper is so valuable and everything.

Americans have come over here and tried to pick up little bits and pieces of John to ... because they know that these archives are interesting and the sort of signs that John has passed this way and has made this observation or picked up a book or a page and done this or that, but nobody, there hasn't been a person doing that because John will all the time be taking it forward into the meanings he's doing with Chris Isham, what is a trajectory, what does it mean?

HUO Everything is in permanent transformation. I mean, rather than classifying a book you use it again and transform it into something else.

BS All these little things.

JL I was over-confident, perhaps, that things which I did would survive, that people would get them. I felt it was obvious that it fitted. Everything which came out was so interesting and it hadn't been done before, it wasn't like anything you could do with a paintbrush, for instance. And you couldn't do it by writing a book. Books were in a different framework in there. I'd got the books saying something which it was somebody else's business to write about, to write up, to decipher. And there isn't anybody who deciphers this thing. So I have taken to writing the interpretation down because I'd had the experience from the 1950s of the two scientists who'd joined, who'd picked up the ball and started to run with it. They made an institute when they first ... when they saw the painting, the marks, they said, 'Oh, cosmological' and founded an Institute for the Study of Mental Images.

HUO Those are your science friends?

JL Professor Gregory and Anita Kohsen ... He was a very distinguished astronomer with a lot of experience in psi research ... he was the founder of the University College Observatory and the Radcliffe Observatory in Oxford, for example.

HUO And his name was Gregory?

JL Clive Gregory. C.C.L. Gregory, if you want to put the whole thing down. And his partner was called Anita Kohsen and she was an ethologist in organic behaviour and they were thought to have betrayed the whole of science by crossing disciplines, making a hybrid. It was not quite the way everything was supposed to go and even now there isn't anybody who's got a good hybrid science. It hadn't been done because it wasn't visualised in event terms, they hadn't got the proper visual. Well, Gregory's had the visual.

HUO It's they who invited you to their house to do this seminal work on the wall?

BS Yes.

HUO Could you tell me the story?

JL Well, I was inventing or rather discovering it as well, because I hadn't used this gizmo before and I had thought about it and I knew I'd got enough in my head to be able to say, 'Well, it'll only take me an hour to do the whole thing, to do it. I don't even need the hour.' It took about a minute, really, to do what they needed. But in those days one hour was quite a lot of time. A work doesn't need much time to finish. Anyway, I was enjoying just finding out what I could do with the kind of mark which came out and what happened if you drew, if you pulled a dry brush across it, the wet point marks. You got an equivalent for what we might think of as solar wind, like information wind for instance, a popular image. You don't see it and we don't know what to say about that kind of effect; information is picked up, gets into people's belief 11:20 systems. The way that information gets around is not carried on radiation waves, it's not wave-formed at all. The form that it does take is event-structural, what we began with.

HUO On the one hand you don't archive books. But on the other hand, you always have books around. Whenever I come to the studio, there's books which are lying around which you use ... you slice them up and you use them.

JL Oh yes.

HUO Are these books you find incidentally or do you have a kind of archive of books which you then use for certain pieces?

JL Well, I find them in several places. Like when I went to Pittsburgh they had got a load of various remaindered kinds from the library. Who was the tycoon, the steel tycoon? Carnegie? Anyway, it was an American steel tycoon who left this library to the town, the city, and they had this lot of spare books which had gone to the Mattress Factory for my use. About 20,000 books, I suppose, all very interesting so I used as many as I wanted, in one way or another, but that didn't make much of an impact on the stack left behind.

BS But sometimes you collect books incidentally, but this Pittsburgh thing ... I'm just going back to get the actual publication about the works.

HUO So the Pittsburgh piece was a sheer quantity of books?

BS It was a sheer quantity of books but John also picked up ... Well, I mean sometimes he will seize on a title like when he made those pieces for Toronto, you know, 36 glass pieces with books across all in a circle in Basel, one title was *Pregnancy Survival Manual*. The feminists got very angry when they saw it being used like that. We had quite a little riot here. But why had he chosen that title, you see? Sometimes the title was very important, other times it's flux ...

HUO Is the book an incidental person?

JL Yes, it can stand there for a person, or a part person, or a rational part person with an irrational part person or connecting up with a source of data which only becomes part of a person when it is intuited. The form of a book is ideally suited to show sculpturally what we never see otherwise, the world is person, if you get to understand the dimensional components I described.

HUO Can it be an incidental person?

JL It's like what informs a person ... a book in the work which is not obviously for reading has to have some more form. It becomes very plastic, a huge variety of forms that you can get out of it. It sort of seems endless to me even though having worked through a lot of it I would say, well, maybe I've finished that for the time being. I then come across a student, like GW, for instance, who's now a well known young lady. She came to me very excited, she said 'I've got, I've just seen your show and I'm working with books, too. I want to come and talk to you about it.' I said, 'I'm the last person you want to talk to if you're working in books. You don't want to familiarise yourself. You want to do what you do without knowing that somebody else has done it.' 'Oh, no', she said, 'I want to come and see you. It's very important.' So I said, 'Well, okay. On your own head be it.' So she came and, of course, I have a few photographs of her book work which she was kind enough to send me, but she never made, she didn't try to run that as her art project. That was what I meant. She didn't ... It wouldn't get anywhere. So it was just as well because she's done something else and it's quite gratifying that she had the guts to invent on the media that she'd found useful, things to say. She'd found things to say out of those things which were available. So I'm pleased with her.

HOU To continue with this incidental person issue how would you define now an incidental person? What's the incidental person?

JL Yes, you need to get this very clear. There are a lot of people who come out of college, who've come out, just grew up and into a world which seems to make sense as making money and being set according to rules. An IP is someone who knows this needs reforming ...

This is the transcription of a video-interview by Hans Ulrich Obrist with John Latham and Barbara Steveni held in July 1999. It was made for the exhibition project *Interarchiv* in Lüneburg, 1997–2002. First published in *Interarchive: Archival Practices and Sites in the Contemporary Art Field*, Cologne: König, 2002.

John Latham Canvas Events 1994

Canvas Event [1], 1994
Spray painted canvas twisted on stretcher
193 × 94 cm | 76 × 37 in

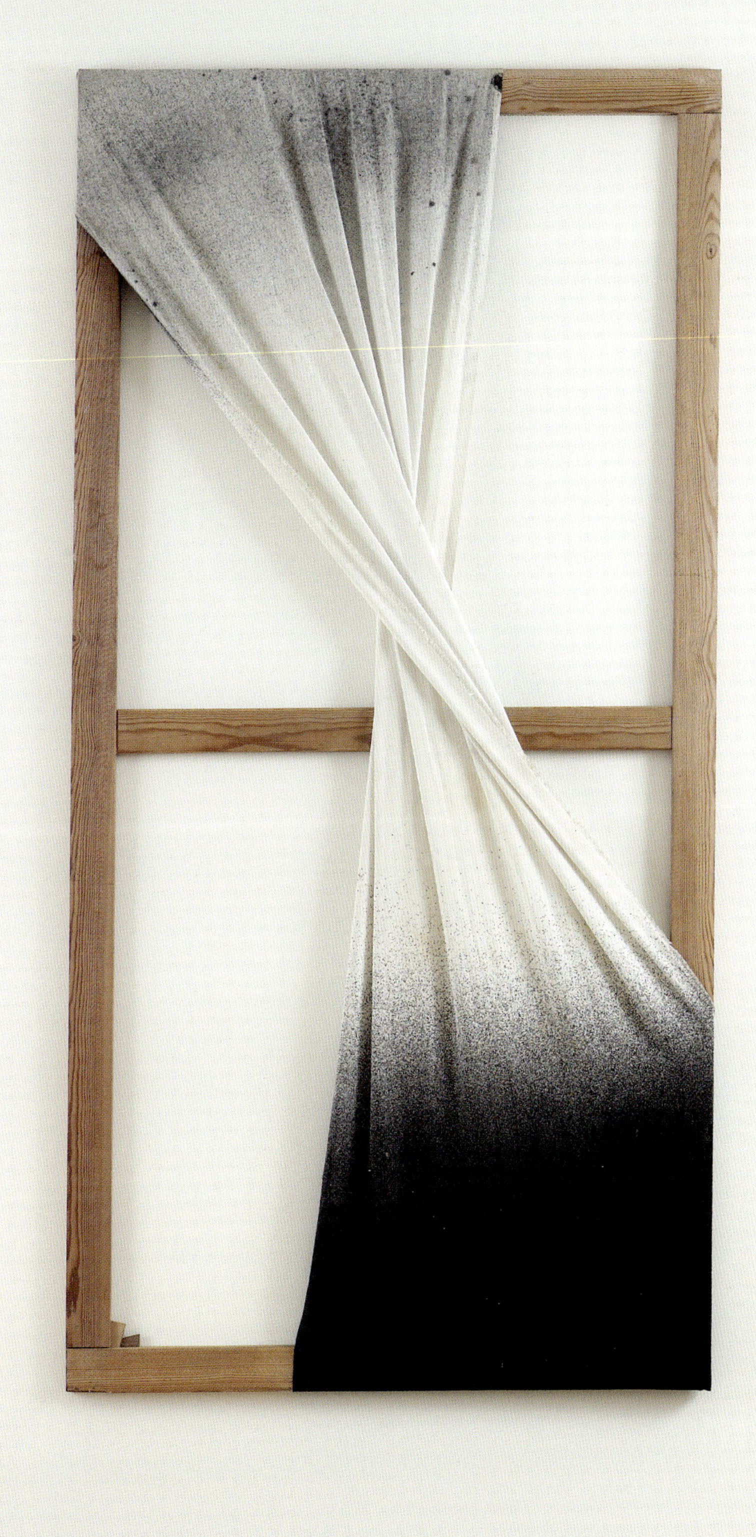

Canvas Event [2], 1994
Spray painted canvas twisted on stretcher
77 × 64 cm | 30½ × 25⅓ in

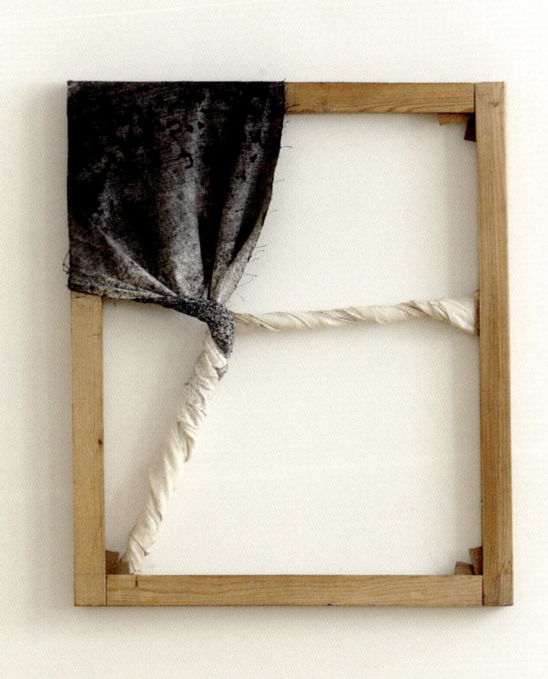

Canvas Event [3], 1994
Spray painted canvas twisted on stretcher
140 × 74 cm | 55⅙ × 29¼ in

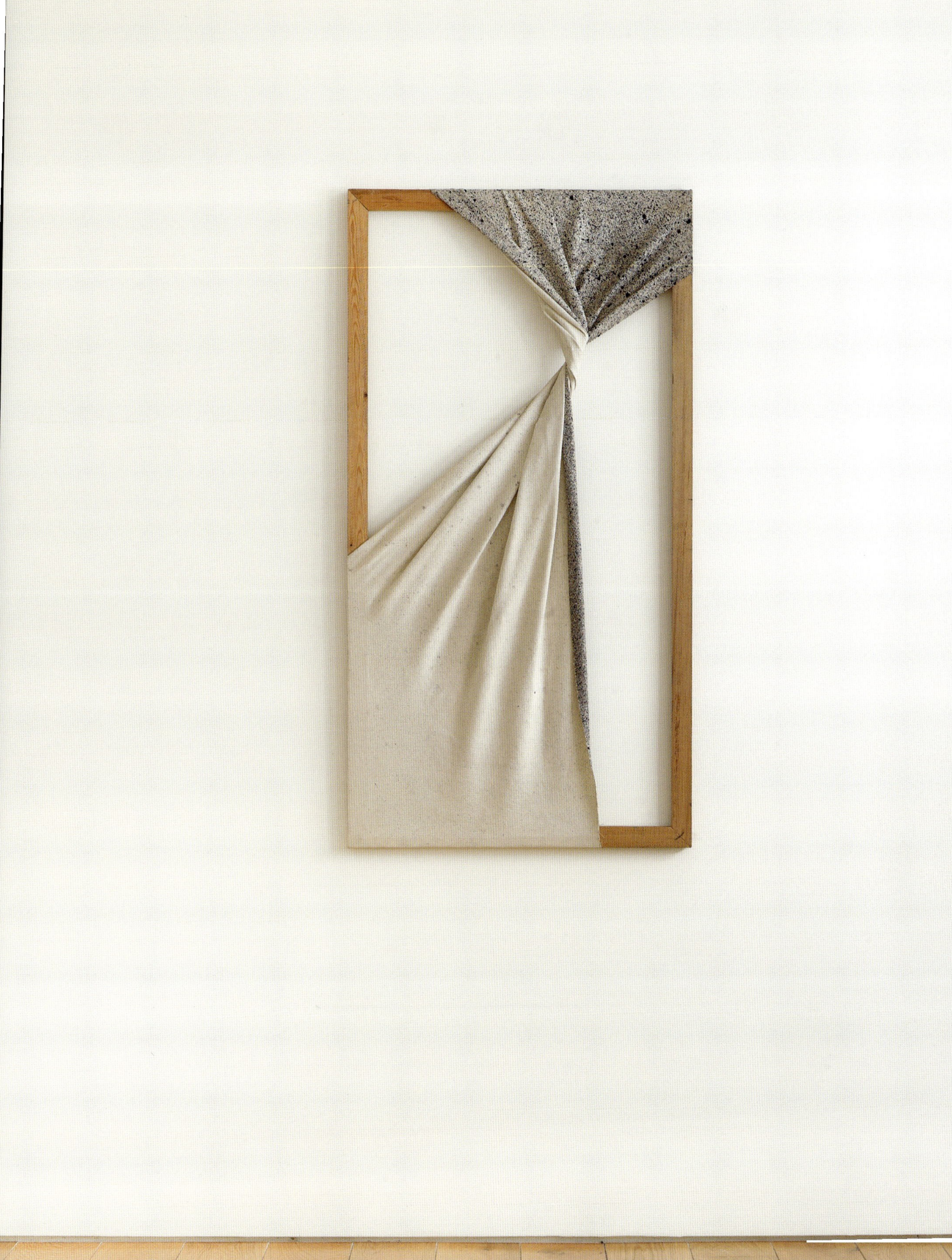

Canvas Event [4], 1994
Spray painted canvas twisted on stretcher
54.7 × 46 cm | 21½ × 18¼ in

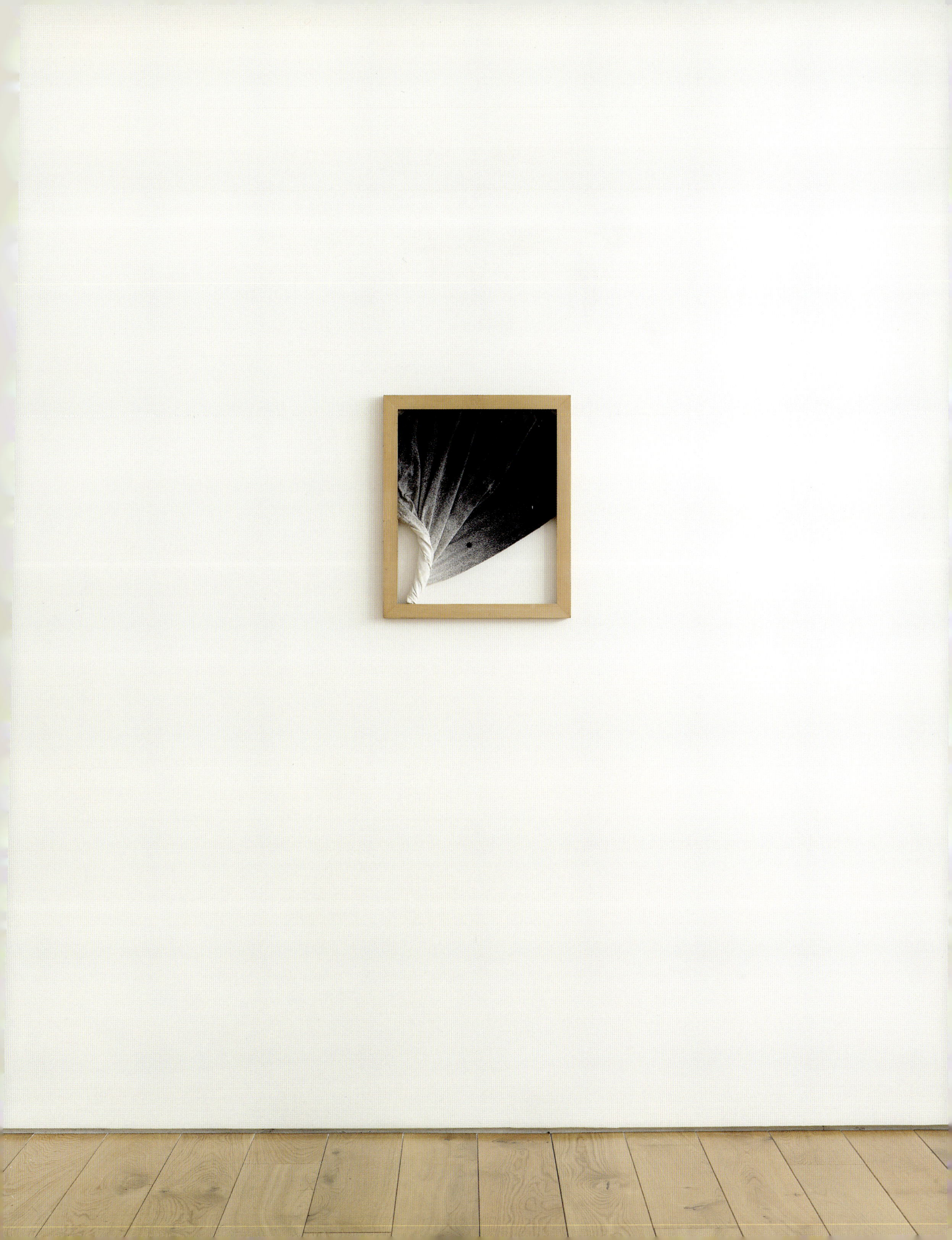

Canvas Event [5], 1994
Spray painted canvas twisted on stretcher
101.6 × 76.3 cm | 40 × 30 in

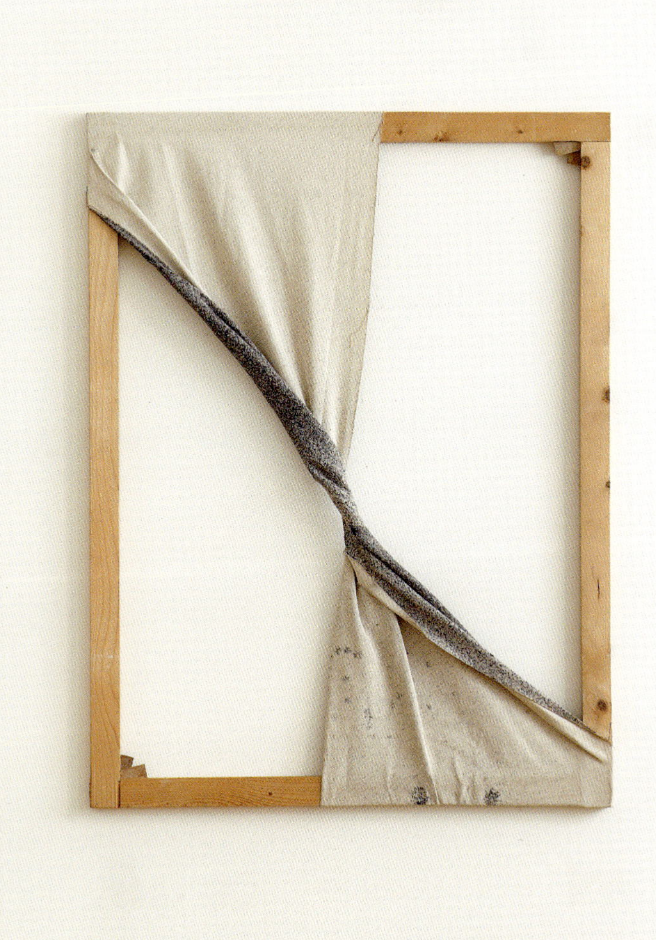

Canvas Event [6], 1994
Spray painted canvas twisted on stretcher
140 × 74.4 cm | 55¼ × 29½ in